Planning for Learning through The senses

by Judith Harries. Illustrated by Cathy Hughes

Contents

Published by Practical Pre-School Books, A Division of MA Education Ltd,
St Jude's Church, Dulwich Road, Herne Hill, London, SE24 0PB Tel: 020 7738 5454

www.practicalpreschoolbooks.com

Revised edition (2nd edition) © MA Education Ltd 2014. First edition © MA Education Limited 2007.

Front and back cover images taken by Lucie Carlier © MA Education Ltd

Planning for Learning through The senses: ISBN: 978-1-909280-63-2

Making plans

Child-friendly planning

The purpose of planning is to make sure that all children enjoy a broad and balanced experience of learning. Planning should be flexible, useful and child-friendly. It should reflect opportunities available both indoors and outside. Plans form part of a planning cycle in which practitioners make observations, assess and plan.

Children benefit from reflective planning that takes into account the children's current interests and abilities and also allows them to take the next steps in their learning. Plans should make provision for activity that promotes learning and a desire to imagine, observe, communicate, experiment, investigate and create.

Plans should include a variety of types of activity. Some will be adult-initiated or adult-led, that focus on key skills or concepts. These should be balanced with opportunities for child-initiated activity where the children take a key role in the planning. In addition there is a need to plan for the on-going continuous provision areas such as construction, sand and water, malleable materials, small world, listening area, role-play and mark-making. Thought also needs to be given to the enhanced provision whereby an extra resource or change may enable further exploration, development and learning.

The outdoor environment provides valuable opportunities for children's learning. It is vital that plans value the use of outdoor space.

The UK Frameworks

Within the UK a number of frameworks exist to outline the provision that children should be entitled to receive. Whilst a variety of terms and labels are used to describe the Areas of Learning there are key principles which are common to each document. For example they advocate that practitioners' planning should be personal based on observations and knowledge of the specific children within a setting. They acknowledge that young children learn best when there is scope for child-initiated activity. In addition it is accepted that young children's learning is holistic. Although within the documents Areas of Learning are presented separately to ensure that key areas are not over-looked, within settings, children's learning will combine areas. Thus the Areas of Learning are perhaps of most use for planning, assessment and recording.

Focused area plans

The plans you make for each day will outline areas of continuous provision and focused, adult-led activities. Plans for focused-area activities need to include aspects such as:

Making plans

- resources needed;
- the way in which you might introduce activities;
- individual needs;
- the organisation of adult help;
- size of the group;
- timing;
- safety;
- key vocabulary.

Identify the learning and the Early Learning Goals that each activity is intended to promote. Make a note of any assessments or observations that you are likely to carry out. After carrying out the activities, make notes on your plans to say what was particularly successful, or any changes you would make another time.

A final note

Planning should be seen as flexible. Not all groups meet every day, and not all children attend every day. Any part of the plan can be used independently, stretched over a longer period or condensed to meet the needs of any group. You will almost certainly adapt the activities as children respond to them in different ways and bring their own ideas, interests and enthusiasms. The important thing is to ensure that the children are provided with a varied and enjoyable curriculum that meets their individual developing needs.

Using the book

Read the section which outlines links to the Early Learning Goals (pages 4-6) and explains the rationale for focusing on 'The senses'.

The chart on page 7 gives an example format for weekly planning. It provides opportunity to plan for the on-going continuous provision, as well as more focused activities.

Use pages 8 to 19 to select from a wide range of themed, focused activities that recognise the importance of involving children in practical activities and giving them opportunities to follow their own interests. For each 'senses' theme, two activities are described in detail as examples to help you in your planning and preparation. Key vocabulary, questions and learning opportunities are identified. Use the activities as a basis to:

- extend current and emerging interests and capabilities
- engage in sustained conversations
- stimulate new interests and skills

Find out on page 20 how 'The senses' activities can be brought together with The senses factory.

Use page 21 for ideas of resources to collect or prepare. Remember that the books listed are only suggestions. It is likely that you will already have within your setting a variety of other books that will be equally useful.

The activity overview chart on page 23 can be used either at the planning stage or after each theme has been completed. It will help you to see at a glance which aspects of children's development are being addressed and alert you to the areas which may need greater input in the future.

As children take part in the activities, their learning will progress. 'Collecting evidence' on page 22 explains how you might monitor each child's achievements.

There is additional material to support the working partnership of families and children in the form of a reproducible Family page found inside the back cover.

It is important to appreciate that the ideas presented in this book will only be a part of your planning. Many activities that will be taking place as routine in your group may not be mentioned. For example, it is assumed that sand, dough, water, puzzles, role-play, floor toys, technology and large scale apparatus are part of the ongoing early years experience. Role-play areas, stories, rhymes, singing, and group discussion times are similarly assumed to be happening in each week although they may not be a focus for described activities.

Using the 'Early Learning Goals'

The principles that are common to each of the United Kingdom curriculum frameworks for the early years are described on page 2. It is vital that, when planning for children within a setting, practitioners are familiar with the relevant framework's content and organisation for areas of learning. Regardless however, of whether a child attends a setting in England, Northern Ireland, Scotland or Wales they have a right to provision for all areas of learning. The children should experience activities which encourage them to develop their communication and language; personal, social, emotional, physical, mathematical and creative skills. They should have opportunities within literacy and be encouraged to understand and explore their world.

Within the Statutory Framework for the Early Years Foundation Stage (2012), Communication and Language; Physical Development and Personal, Social and Emotional Development are described as Prime Areas of Learning that are 'particularly crucial for igniting children's curiosity and enthusiasm for learning, and for building their capacity to learn, form relationships and thrive' (page 4, DfE 2012). The Specific Areas of Learning are Literacy, Mathematics, Understanding the World and Expressive Arts and Design.

For each Area of Learning the Early Learning Goals (ELGs) describe what children are expected to be able to do by the time they enter Year 1. These goals, detailed on pages 4 to 6, have been used throughout this book to show how activities relating to 'The senses' could link to these expectations. For example, for Personal, Social and Emotional Development, one aim relates to the development of children's 'self-confidence and self-awareness'. Activities suggested which provide the opportunity for children to do this have the reference PSE1. This will enable you to see which parts of the Early Learning Goals are covered for a given theme and to plan for areas to be revisited and developed.

In addition, an activity may be carried out to develop a range of different Early Learning Goals. For example, when the children make menus of favourite foods for the Tasty cafe they will develop their writing skills for Literacy. Also, when they write with a good pencil hold, they will use their fine motor skills alongside gaining understanding of a healthy diet which are both part of Physical Development. Thus, whilst adult-focused activities may have clearly defined goals at the planning stage, it must be remembered that as children take on ideas and initiate their own learning and activities, goals may change.

The Prime Areas of Learning

Communication and Language

Listening and attention: children listen attentively in a range of situations. They listen to stories, accurately anticipating key events and respond to what they hear with relevant comments, questions or actions. They give their attention to what others say and respond appropriately, while engaged in another activity. (CL1)

Understanding: children follow instructions involving several ideas or actions. They answer 'how' and 'why' questions about their experiences and in response to stories or events. (CL2)

Speaking: children express themselves effectively, showing awareness of listeners' needs. They use past, present and future forms accurately when talking about events that have happened or are to happen in the future. They develop their own narratives and explanations by connecting ideas or events. (CL3)

'The senses' provides many opportunities for children to enjoy listening, understanding and speaking. There are a wide range of books featuring The senses and these can be used to stimulate interest in the chosen themes, encouraging children to listen and to talk. When discussing losing things and favourite sights, sounds and smells, children will have the opportunity to ask questions. Setting up and using role-play areas such as the opticians will allow the children to follow instructions and develop their own narratives. Playing 'The cuckoo song', using the giant feely box and making up stories for others to listen to, will encourage children to express themselves and to show awareness of listeners' needs.

Physical Development

Moving and handling: children show good control and co-ordination in large and small movements. They move confidently in a range of ways, safely negotiating space. They handle equipment and tools effectively, including pencils for writing. (PD1)

Health and self-care: children know the importance for good health of physical exercise, and a healthy diet, and talk about ways to keep healthy and safe. They manage their own basic hygiene and personal needs successfully, including dressing and going to the toilet independently. (PD2)

'The senses' offers many opportunities for children to enjoy movement activities and to handle tools and equipment. When children play 'Blindfold pairs' and 'The Elephant' games they develop and demonstrate control and co-ordination. Throwing and catching balls and bean bags, handling textured dough, building walls with boxes, will allow children to use small equipment and promote the development of fine motor skills. In addition, any of the described literacy activities where children write will also contribute to the development of 'handling' skills. Independent dressing skills are practised as part of exploring 'touch'. Areas such as basic hygiene and going to the toilet independently, however, will be part of on-going, daily activity.

Personal, Social and Emotional Development

Self-confidence and self-awareness: children are confident to try new activities, and say why they like some activities more than others. They are confident to speak in a familiar group, will talk about their ideas, and will choose the resources they need for their chosen activities. They say when they do or don't need help. (PSE1)

Managing feelings and behaviour: children talk about how they and others show feelings, talk about their own and others' behaviour, and its consequences, and know that some behaviour is unacceptable. They work as part of a group or class, and understand and follow the rules. They adjust their behaviour to different situations, and take changes of routine in their stride. (PSE2)

Making relationships: children play co-operatively, taking turns with others. They take account of one another's ideas about how to organise their activity. They show sensitivity to others' needs and feelings, and form positive relationships with adults and other children. (PSE3)

'The senses' offers many opportunities, both for child-initiated and adult-led activities, which will develop children personally, socially and emotionally. Considering the need to say 'please' and 'thank you' when visiting the Opticians or the Tasty cafe, or treating visitors with visual or hearing impairments with respect, gives children the opportunity to consider acceptable behaviour. Collaborating to 'pass a sound around', use sign language, going on a listening and touching walk, will encourage children to make relationships. Many of the areas described within the ELGs for Personal, Social and Emotional Development though, will be covered on an almost incidental basis. Any activity that involves making choices, or showing initiative, will promote self-confidence and self-awareness.

The Specific Areas of Learning
Literacy

Reading: children read and understand simple sentences. They use phonic knowledge to decode regular words and read them aloud accurately. They also read some common irregular words. They demonstrate understanding when talking with others about what they have read. (L1)

Writing: children use their phonic knowledge to write words in ways which match their spoken sounds. They also write some irregular common words. They write simple sentences which can be read by themselves and others. Some words are spelt correctly and others are phonetically plausible. (L2)

Activities for 'The senses', based on picture books and stories, will provide opportunities for the children to read using both their phonic knowledge and memories of common, irregular words. Discussions of the stories will help children to understand and to develop their vocabularies. Activities such as making Braille letters, creating a book about My Senses, and writing in trays of sand or other materials, will encourage children to explore the sounds within words and to enjoy the early stages of writing.

Mathematics

Numbers: children count reliably with numbers from 1 to 20, place them in order and say which number is one more or one less than a given number. Using quantities and objects, they add and subtract two single-digit numbers and count on or back to find the answer. They solve problems, including doubling, halving and sharing. (M1)

Shape, space and measures: children use everyday language to talk about size, weight, capacity, position, distance, time and money to compare quantities and objects and to solve problems. They recognise, create and describe patterns. They explore characteristics of everyday objects and shapes and use mathematical language to describe them. (M2)

Activities for 'The senses' provide many opportunities for children to count, to measure and to explore shape and space. Going on a treasure hunt, playing 'Number soundtracks', and singing number rhymes encourage children to count and to compare. Making fruit kebabs, playing 'Eat the pie' and making lift the flap books helps the children to develop awareness of shape and pattern. Following recipes, making favourite foods and matching pairs of sounds and textures increases children's awareness of sizes and measurements.

Understanding the World

People and communities: children talk about past and present events in their own lives and in the lives of family members. They know that other children don't always enjoy the same things, and are sensitive to this. They know about similarities and differences between themselves and others, and among families, communities and traditions. (UW1)

The world: children know about similarities and differences in relation to places, objects, materials and living things. They talk about the features of their own immediate environment and how environments might vary from one another. They make observations of Food and plants and explain why some things occur, and talk about changes. (UW2)

Technology: children recognise that a range of technology is used in places such as homes and schools. They select and use technology for particular purposes. (UW3)

To understand their world children need times to gain knowledge, to explore and to relate what they discover to both previously held ideas and future learning. When exploring different smells and tastes, children will be able to make comparisons and notice similarities and differences. Looking at how the eyes and ears work and how different senses operate encourages children to investigate and ask questions. When children search for information about senses, and investigate fingerprints they have the opportunity to use technology. Technology will also feature in role play as well as being part of the on-going, daily provision. Discussions with visitors about visual and hearing impairment will provide opportunity to consider events from the past, the present and the future.

Expressive Arts and Design

Exploring and using media and materials: children sing songs, make music and dance, and experiment with ways of changing them. They safely use and explore a variety of materials, tools and techniques, experimenting with colour, design, texture, form and function. (EAD1)

Being imaginative: children use what they have learnt about media and materials in original ways, thinking about uses and purposes. They represent their own ideas, thoughts and feelings through design and technology, art, music, dance, role-play and stories. (EAD2)

Whilst involved in activities around 'The senses', children will experience working with a variety of materials, tools and techniques as they make ink blot pictures, press prints, use perfumed paint and create Touch squares. When creating fancy spectacles, painting to music, collages of favourite food, and making musical instruments, children have the chance to be imaginative. Throughout all the activities children should be encouraged to talk about what they see and feel as they communicate their ideas in painting, model making, music and role play.

Note

The Early Learning Goals raise awareness of key aspects within any child's development for each Area of Learning. It is important to remember that these goals are reached through a combination of adult and child-initiated activity within Early Years settings and also a child's home life. Thus, it is vital that goals are shared by practitioners and parents, and children are given every opportunity to develop throughout their Early Years Foundation Stage at home and within a setting.

Week beginning:	Monday	Tuesday	Wednesday	Thursday	Friday
FOCUSED ACTIVITIES					
Focus Activity 1:					
Focus Activity 2:					
Stories and rhymes					
CONTINUOUS PROVISION (Indoor)					
Collage					
Construction (large)					
Construction (small)					
ICT					
Imaginative play					
Listening					
Malleable materials					
Mark making					
Painting					
Role play					
Sand (damp)					
Sand (dry)					
Water					
CONTINUOUS PROVISION (Outdoor)					
Construction					
Creative play					
Exploratory play					
Gross motor					
ENHANCED PROVISION (Indoor)					
ENHANCED PROVISION (Outdoor)					

Theme 1: Seeing eyes

Be sensitive to children in your group who have visual impairment and adapt activities where necessary so that every child feels included.

Communication and Language
- Introduce the theme by inviting a child to lie down on a large piece of paper and then draw round their shape. Discuss and label the different body parts in relation to the senses. (CL1, 2)
- Set up an opticians in the role-play area (see activity opposite). (CL2, 3)
- Read some 'lift the flap' books such as *Duck's Key, Where can it be?* by Jez Alborough or *Where's Spot?* by Eric Hill. Make up some new stories about losing something important and having to look everywhere to find it. (CL1, 2, 3)

Physical Development
- Play 'Blindfold pairs'. Ask children to work with a partner. Blindfold one of the pair and ask the sighted partner to guide their friend around the equipment. Then swap over. (PD1, 2)
- Practise throwing and catching with different-sized balls, skittles, quoits and bean bags. Remind the children to keep their eye on the ball! (PD1)

Personal, Social and Emotional Development
- Play a circle game of 'I spy'. Use colours, shapes, sizes as well as initial letters. (PSE1, 3)
- Invite a partially sighted or blind person to visit with their guide dog and talk to the children. Talk about what it might feel like to not be able to see. Which activities would it be difficult to do? If possible, look at some Braille books. Use embossed stamps and coins to make raised patterns. (PSE2, 3)
- Read *Lucy's Picture* by Nicola Moon. How did Lucy help her blind Grandpa to see her picture? Make textured pictures to say thank you to your blind visitor or to give to a local RNIB group. (PSE3)

Literacy
- Make a class book of 'My senses', beginning this week with sight, and add to it throughout the topic. Ask children to draw or cut out pictures of eyes and label them. Help them to write simple sentences about their favourite sights. (L2)
- Let children make their own Braille initial letters. Push pencil into a reversed letter shape until it makes a small hole or indent. Repeat along whole letter shape. Turn over and trace the letter shape with a finger. Can they read the letter? (L1, 2)

Mathematics
- Go on a treasure hunt outside. Give children a list of things to find or spot such as:

3 stones	2 birds
1 feather	4 windows
5 leaves	1 flower

  Can they find one more stone? How many have they got altogether? (M1)
- Try some estimating activities (see activity opposite). (M1)
- Make a lift the flap picture using numbers. Draw some small pictures of groups of minibeasts, flowers, shapes, or smiley faces. Cover each picture with a flap. How many faces can the children find? (M1, 2)
- Play a game with a hand puppet and a set of coloured cards. Use three pairs of red, yellow and blue cards. If the puppet holds up one colour, ask the children to find the matching pair and shout 'snap'! Try the game with matching shape and number cards 1-20. Hide one card. Can the children tell which number or shape is missing? (M1, 2)

Understanding the World
- Ask children to look carefully at each other's eyes and their own eyes using hand mirrors. Show them a diagram of the eye and talk about how it works. What do eyelashes do? Why do some people need to wear glasses or contact lenses? (UW2)
- Make a collection of tools used for looking at things, such as mirrors, magnifying glasses, a digital microscope, visualiser, binoculars, telescope, and so on. Help children use them to see how they work. (UW2, 3)
- Make pretend binoculars out of pairs of cardboard tubes. (UW2)

Expressive Arts and Design
- Sing verse one of this 'Senses song' to the tune of 'In and out the bluebells':
  With my two eyes, I can see (x3)
  Using all my senses.
  Add new verses each week, for example: 'With my two ears, I can hear' and so on. (EAD1)
- Make ink-blot paintings. Drop a pool of very runny paint onto paper and blow with straws to make new shapes. What can the children see? Can they turn it into something new? (EAD2)

- Make fancy spectacles. Cut templates for children to decorate with paint, sequins, beads, feathers, lace, ribbon, netting, fabric, and shiny paper. Display them at the opticians. (EAD2)

Activity: The opticians

Learning opportunity: Using the role-play corner to share and explore experiences. Writing letters, shapes, colours and numbers and using ICT to make eye charts.

Early Learning Goal: Communication and Language. Speaking.

Resources: A role-play area set out as an opticians (with a chair, lots of glasses frames, mirrors, torch, computer, telephone, eye charts, posters and brochures about glasses and contact lenses); card; pens; pencils; children's name cards.

Organisation: Whole group introduction with small group using the area.

Key vocabulary: Opticians, eyes, sight, see, letters, numbers, shapes, colours.

What to do: Talk about going to the opticians for an eye test.

Invite any children who have visited the opticians to share their experiences.

Involve children in setting up the area. Ask them to make eye charts using lower case and capital letters, simple outline shapes, blocks of colour or numbers. Can they make the rows of letters or shapes start big and get smaller as they move down the page? Use a computer to allow children to change the style and size of fonts.

Talk about how to use the area. Show children how to try on glasses and read the charts. Warn children not to shine lights or put anything in their eyes – only pretend! Encourage them to take turns at different roles: optician, patient, friend, receptionist.

Activity: How many?

Learning opportunity: Developing, estimating and counting skills.

Early Learning Goal: Mathematics. Numbers.

Resources: Cubes; sweets; raisins; glass pebbles; different-sized boxes; weights; weighing scales.

Organisation: Small group.

Key vocabulary: Estimate, guess, count, more, less, heaviest, lightest, same, tallest, measure.

What to do: Show children some cubes (start with under ten) and let them hold them in their hands. Can they guess how many there are? Count the cubes to find out if they are right. Try again with more cubes. Put some glass pebbles on a plate or sweets or raisins in a jar and ask children to estimate how many there are. Do they think there are more or less than ten? Help them to count and check.

Fill a set of different-sized boxes with a variety of weights. Can they tell which is the heaviest just by looking? Let them pick up the boxes and estimate again. Weigh boxes to establish their weights. Begin by making the biggest box heaviest, and the smallest the lightest. Then mix up the contents and try again. The children will find out that they cannot rely on just sight.

Display

On a display table, make a collection of fiction and non-fiction books about senses. Add posters, puzzles and games. This week include lift-the-flap books and those with things to spot! Compile a list of useful words about the senses and display them around the room.

Make a bar chart of eye colours in the group. Help children to cut out pictures of eyes from magazines to stick on the chart. Which is the most common colour?

Under a heading 'What can you see?' leave out the microscope and magnifying glasses for children to use. Provide some magnifying up pots and bugs for them to observe.

Theme 2: Hearing ears

Be sensitive to children in your group who have a hearing impairment and adapt activities where necessary so that every child feels included.

Communication and Language

- Record the children talking and singing. Can they recognise themselves or identify each other's voices? Play 'The cuckoo song'. Sit in a circle and ask for a volunteer to sit in the middle wearing a blindfold. Hide a small soft toy bird behind another child's back. All sing 'Cuckoo, where are you?' The child with the toy replies 'cuckoo'. Can the blindfolded child recognise who sang? (CL1, 3)
- Make a cosy listening area with comfortable chairs and cushions. Encourage children to listen to stories or music on a computer, tablet or CD player. Invite them to talk to the group about they heard. (CL1, 3)

Physical Development

- Play 'Musical moves' (see activity opposite). (PD1)
- Hide a loudly ticking clock in the room for a volunteer to find. Alternatively, invite a child to hide outside and blow a whistle regularly. Ask the other children to be very quiet so the seeker can hear the sounds. (PD1, 2)

Personal, Social and Emotional Development

- Go on a listening walk inside and outside the setting. Can children identify al the sounds they hear? Were there any unexpected sounds? (PSE1, 2)
- Pass a sound around the circle. Take it in turns to make a sound using voice, body percussion or instruments. (PSE1, 3)
- How easy is it to create silence? Imagine what it would be like to not be able to hear any sounds. Teach some simple sign language. Hello – a simple wave from the forehead outwards. Go to www.britishsignlanguage.com and learn some more signs. Try singing a song using sign language. (PSE1, 2, 3)

Literacy

- Invite children to read books to each other in the cosy listening area. (L1)
- Play a circle game 'I hear with my little ear, something that rhymes with...'. Make a collection of words that rhyme with 'hear'. Make rhyming word chains for other senses words and hang them up on the wall. Change game to 'I hear with my little ear, a word that starts with 'B' and make a list of 'B' words.

- Hold a large shell up to the children's ears and invite them to listen carefully. What can they hear? Help them to write imaginative poems called 'Inside the shell'. (L2)

Mathematics

- Play 'Number soundtracks'. Record a series of number questions on a tablet for children to listen to and explore, such as 'Which number comes after four?'; 'Point at number seven'; and 'Which number is one less than three'? Can they make up some new number puzzles for each other? (M1)
- Make a set of matching sound pots. You will need five pairs of black and white film cannisters or small plastic pots. Fill with coins, rice, beans, sand and lentils. Can children find the matching pairs just by shaking and listening? (M1)
- Play 'Can you remember?' Sit in a circle with a group of musical instruments in the middle. Invite a child to choose an instrument to play. Ask them to make a sound on the instrument and then get the next child to repeat it and add one of their own. How many sounds can they remember? (M1)

Understanding the World

- Investigate how our ears work (see activity opposite). (UW2)
- Make a telephone using two plastic cups and a length of string pulled taut. Give children messages to send to each other. What happens if the string is not stretched? Press a plastic funnel into the end of a length of plastic tubing or hose pipe and make a listening tube. Which works best? (UW2)

Expressive Arts and Design

- Sing the 'Sound song' from *Game Songs with Prof. Dogg's Troupe*. Help children to echo sounds using voices, body percussion and musical instruments. (EAD1)
- Make sounds for children to guess using things around the room or body sounds. Go behind a screen or ask them to shut their eyes so they can concentrate on listening. Try clapping hands, shaking keys, tearing paper, bouncing a ball, tapping a pencil on a table, stamping feet on the floor. Invite children to make sounds for the others to identify. (EAD1)
- Try drawing and painting to music. Choose contrasting moods of music to inspire different styles of painting. (EAD2)

Activity: How do your ears work?

Learning opportunity: Investigating how well our ears work in different situations.

Early Learning Goal: Understanding the World. The world.

Resources: *The Best Ears in the World* by Claire Llewellyn (optional); diagram of the inner ear; cardboard; scissors; sticky tape; blindfold; drum; rice; triangle.

Organisation: Whole group for circle game and book, small groups for investigations.

Key vocabulary: Ears, sounds, vibrate, drum, near, faraway, safe, danger.

What to do: Sit in a circle and play Chinese whispers. Does the message stay the same as it passes from ear to ear? How does the ear hear the sounds?

Look at a diagram of the inner ear and point out the eardrum and all the tiny bones. Put a few grains of rice on the drum skin and ask a child to tap the drum gently. Watch the rice jump up and down as the drum vibrates. Explain that this creates a sound wave that travels through the air to our ears, along the tiny bones to the eardrum which also vibrates.

Read *The Best Ears in the World*. Investigate how far away we can hear sounds. Ask a child to go to the other end of the room and whisper a message. Who can hear what was said? Help children to make ear trumpets from cones of cardboard. Do they make it easier to hear the whisper?

Go outside with a small group of children and a triangle. Ask a child to play the triangle nearby and then move away five steps and play it again. Keep doing this until the other children cannot hear the sound any more. Try with other sounds. Does everybody hear the same?

Activity: Musical moves

Learning opportunity: Playing cooperatively together and using sounds and music to develop movement and coordination.

Early Learning Goal: Physical Development. Moving and handling.

Resources: Large space; percussion instruments; music for different moods, such as Barber's *Adagio for Strings*, blues songs (sad); Holst's *Jupiter, Turkish Rondo*, (Mozart), dance music (happy); *Moonlight Sonata* (Beethoven), music by Philip Glass (calm); *Mars* (Holst), Stravinsky's *Rite of Spring* (angry); *Five pieces for Orchestra* (Webern), *Danse Macabre* (Saint Saen), some film music/soundtracks (scary) (all available on www.youtube.com).

Organisation: Whole group.

Key vocabulary: Skip, run, hop, freeze, mood, sad, happy, calm, angry, scary.

What to do: Ask children to find a space in the room and stand completely still.

Introduce the different sound signals and invite children to suggest movements for each sound, such as triangle – skip, shaken maraca – run, tapping claves – hop, bang on the tambourine – freeze!

Practise moving when they hear each sound and freezing in-between each movement.

Try making a sequence of sounds and moves for them to copy. Invite children to make sounds for each other.

Develop the game by introducing mood music. Work with children to create happy, sad, calm, angry and scary movements and dances. Perform the dances to other children. Can they identify the moods?

Display

Make an interactive display. Record children's favourite sounds on a tablet. Provide headphones for others to listen to the sounds. Create a giant collage using drawings and paintings of ears and photos cut out of magazines.

Mount the children's shell poems in shell shapes and display around the room. Hang the shell up so others can listen to the sounds inside!

Theme 3: Touching hands

Communication and Language
- Explore a variety of touch books such as Usborne's *Touchy-feely Books*. Make your own class book about favourite things to touch, such as animals (fun fur), warm towel after bath time (towelling), sandpit (sand paper), squidgy dough (piece of dough sealed in cling-film), presents (bubble wrap), and so on. (CL2, 3)
- Make a giant feely box. Cover each side of a cube with a different texture such as velvet, corrugated card, sandpaper, silver foil, wool, lace, plastic, leather, bubble wrap, and so on. Make a hole in one side of the box and put in different items for children to identify by touch. Can they describe what they are feeling for others to guess? (CL3)

Physical Development
- Make play dough or salt and flour dough. Add beans, lentils, pasta, buttons or sequins to change the texture. Press different items such as tools, shells, buttons, and leaves into the dough to make patterns. (PD1)
- Ask children to find a partner and sing 'We all clap hands together' from *This Little Puffin*. Invite children to clap their own hands and then their partners hands. Change actions to shake hands, tap shoulders, rub noses, have a hug, and so on. (PD1)
- Sit down facing a friend and sing to the tune of 'Row, row the boat':
    Hold, hold, hold my hands
    Rocking to and fro,
    Backwards and forwards,
    Round the world we go. (PD1)
- Practise dressing skills. How many children can fasten their own coat or put on their own shoes? Make a chart to encourage children to succeed in dressing themselves. (PD2)

Personal, Social and Emotional Development
- Make a touch board with rough sand paper on one half and a smooth polished surface on the other. Invite children to take turns to feel the contrast with their eyes closed. (PSE1)
- Go on a touching walk outside. Use fingers to feel different textures – floors, walls, pavements, bricks, manhole covers, tree bark, and so on. Make rubbings to record the different feel and patterns. (PSE1, 3)

Literacy
- Practise writing names in shallow trays of dry or wet sand. Use fingers to make patterns and letter shapes.

Try with different materials such as lentils, mud, custard powder, shaving foam, cornflour and water. (L2)
- Collect words to describe touch and textures – hot, cold, wet, dry, rough, smooth, soft, hard, fluffy, sticky, bumpy, and so on. Scribe them on different types of paper shaped like bricks and build a texture wall. (L1, 2)
- Make textured letters or numbers for children to trace with their fingers. Try fun fur, sand paper, bubble wrap, lace, corrugated card, knitted wool, embossed wall paper, and so on. (L1, 2)

Mathematics
- Put ten wooden cubes and ten round beads in a small cloth bag. Ask children to sort them into two piles or sets without looking. Repeat with four shells, four coins, four buttons and four dice. (M1, 2)
- Make a collection of paired objects, such as bottle tops, paper clips, marbles, stones, cubes, shapes, buttons and acorns. Take two bags and put one of each object into a bag. Ask children to find matching pairs. One child picks an object from their bag and their partner has to find the pair. No peaking! Try it with gloves on! Does that make it harder? (M1, 2)
- Try completing tray and shape puzzles wearing a blindfold. (M2)

Understanding the World
- Investigate which part of the body is most sensitive to touch (see activity opposite). (UW2)
- Look at fingerprints under a magnifying glass and observe how they are all different. Can they see the whorl, loop or arch shapes? Use lipstick or paint to create finger prints. Blow them up on a photocopier and compare the patterns. Alternatively, make a thick black mark with a pencil on a piece of a paper. Ask children to press their index finger onto the mark and rock it from side to side. Place a piece of sticky tape onto the finger and lift off gently revealing a print. (UW2, 3)

Expressive Arts and Design
- Mix washing-up liquid into paint to make thick finger paint. Let children enjoy the feel of it on their thumbs and fingers. Make textured paint by adding sand or lentils. Encourage the use of a single thumb and finger prints as well as whole hands. (EAD1, 2)
- Try press printing with different natural and made objects, such as sponges, corks, plastic bricks, shells, pine cones, fruit and vegetables. (EAD1)
- Make 'Touch squares' (see activity opposite). (EAD1)

Planning
for Learning
through
The senses

Activity: Can you feel it?

Learning opportunity: Investigating which part of the body is most sensitive to touch.

Early Learning Goal: Understanding the World. The world.

Resources: Feathers; paper clips; felt pens; paper; pencils; blindfold.

Organisation: Small group.

Key vocabulary: Feel, touch, tickle, palm, back, hand, cheek, arm, leg.

What to do: Explain to children that you are going to find out which parts of the body are most sensitive to touch. Ask them to work with a partner and tickle each other with a feather on the palm and back of the hand. Try the cheek, ear, arm and leg. Which place feels the most ticklish? Is everyone the same?

Use a paper clip bent into a 'U' shape with the tips 2cm apart. Ask children to close their eyes and touch them on the palm of the hand. Can they feel one or two points touch them? Push the points closer together until they can feel only one point. Try on the arm or leg. The more sensitive parts of the body should still feel two points even when they are very close together. Record the results on a chart.

Play 'How close was that?'. Ask for a volunteer to wear a blindfold. Gently touch their hand with a red pen and make a mark. Ask them to use a contrasting colour pen and touch the same place. Remove the blindfold. How close together are the spots? Try again on different parts of the body.

Activity: Touch squares

Learning opportunity: Using a variety of materials to create a 3D patchwork collage.

Early Learning Goal: Expressive Arts and Design. Exploring and using media and materials.

Resources: Stiff cardboard or plywood cut into 30cm squares; straws; lolly sticks; collage materials (such as cotton wool balls, feathers, sand, rocks, twigs, wood, paper, fabric, beans, pasta, string, wool, rice, leaves, silver foil); glue; spray varnish.

Organisation: Small group.

Key vocabulary: Square, touch, names of materials, shiny, smooth, rough, soft, hard, cold, scratchy, tickly, blindfold.

What to do: Allow children time to handle all the different materials and investigate the textures they like. Invite them to bring in suitable materials from home. Ask them to select a variety of contrasting textures to include in their collage boxes.

Help children to prepare the squares by subdividing them into six or nine smaller squares using art straws or lolly sticks. Ask children to stick a different texture into each square. Can they find words to describe each small square?

Ask for a volunteer to wear a blindfold. Can they identify the different materials in a friend's touch square using just their sense of touch?

Display

Make a collection of interesting natural objects to touch such as shells, stones, leaves, fur, leather and sponge. Invite children to handle them carefully and label with suitable describing words. Under the title 'What's inside?' make another collection of things which have a different texture on the outside from the inside (such as crusty bread, oranges, coconuts, soft-centred sweets, bananas, cherries and eggs). Ask children to write double-sided labels describing the textures. For example, 'On the outside I am hard, on the inside I am soft'.

Build a giant patchwork touch wall using the children's touch squares or cut out brick shapes and decorate them with different textures. Print thin borders for the displays using hand and foot prints.

Theme 4: Smelling noses

Communication and Language

- Read *The Smelly Book* by Babette Cole. Enjoy talking about the different smells described in the book. Talk about smells the children like and don't like. (CL1, 3)
- Make some posters about most and least popular smells (see UW). (CL3)
- Make a class 'Smelly book' with scratch and sniff pages using dried herbs (such as oregano, basil, rosemary, mint) or spices (cumin, cinnamon, cloves) and dried flowers. (CL2, 3)

Physical Development

- Move around the room like elephants (see activity opposite). (PD1)
- Go on a smelling walk, inside and outside. Talk about nice and nasty smells. Can children recognise all the smells? Try to smell flowers, leaves, fresh air, traffic fumes, dustbins, fresh laundry, cooking, rain, soap, and so on. (PD1, 2)
- Try some deep breathing exercises. Stand up tall, breathe in and out slowly. Try holding breath for a count of five. To help children breathe in properly, ask them to pretend to sniff a sweet flower or a cup of hot chocolate. What happens if you ask them to sniff a smelly sock or mouldy tomato? They could breathe out quickly and pull a disgusted face! Ask them to run around the room until you give them a signal to stop. What has happened to their breathing now? (PD1, 2)

Personal, Social and Emotional Development

- Read *The Three Little Wolves and the Big Bad Pig* by Eugene Trivizas. Talk about how this story differs from the traditional 'Three little pigs' version. How do the nice smells help the pig become good? (PSE2)
- Talk about how our sense of smell can warn us of possible dangers and keep us safe. What would the children do if they smelled smoke? If something smells bad, should they eat or drink it? (PSE1, 2)
- Organise a 'Smelly Socks Day' (see activity opposite). (PSE1)

Literacy

- Write a group poem entitled 'I like the smell of...'. Talk about favourite smells to use in the poem, such as fresh air, clean clothes, fresh bread, cake, chocolate, flowers,

peppermint. Change to nasty smells, such as dirty socks, medicine, toilets, wet hair, burnt toast, coffee. Do the children agree on which smells they like and don't like? Help them to use phonic knowledge to write words. (L2)

Mathematics

- Make smelly play dough following this recipe:
  2 cups of flour   Food colouring
  2 cups of water   3 tsp cream of tartar
  1 cup of salt   1 tbsp veg. oil
  2 drops of one of these: peppermint oil, carnation or other flower oil, orange oil, mixed spice or cinnamon. Heat all the ingredients in a saucepan, stirring until they blend into a thick dough. Use number cards and ask children to make two flowers, four gingerbread men, and so on. (M1, 2)
- Make a bar chart of most and least favourite smells. Which is the most popular? (M1)
- Let children make smelly spells and potions in the water tray using safe herbs and spices (such as cinnamon, cumin, ginger, mixed spice), coloured water, different-sized bottles with lids, teaspoons, pipettes, bowls and so on. Can they name, label and price their creations? (M1, 2)

Understanding the World

- Make a collection of strong smells for the children to sniff. Can they recognise lemon, banana, mint, garlic, chocolate, coffee, roses, pencil shavings, vinegar, sawdust, ginger? Ask them to close their eyes or use a blindfold. Which smells do they like and not like? (UW2)

- Play 'Smelly matching pairs'. Put matching smells in plastic lidded containers. Can the children find two that smell the same? (UW2)
- Read *Whose Nose and Toes?* by John Butler. Draw and paint pictures of animals with special noses and toes! (UW2)

Expressive Arts and Design

- Add perfume, bathoil, aromatherapy oil, coffee or spices to paint. (Discourage children from sniffing harmful substances.) Do their paintings still smell when they are dry? (EAD1)
- Make a potpourri using a selection of materials such as coloured pasta, lavender, pine cones, wood shavings, dried flowers, bay leaves, rosemary, dried citrus peel and aromatherapy oils. Put into small plastic bags and fasten with ribbons. Give these to parents and carers as gifts. (EAD1)

Activity: Smelly socks day

Learning opportunity: Sharing the benefit of wearing clean clothes, washing socks and polishing shoes.

Early Learning Goal: Personal, Social and Emotional Development. Self-confidence and self-awareness.

Resources: Children's own pairs of dirty socks; water tray; mild soap powder; rubber gloves; washing line; pegs; washboard; mangle; ironing board; iron; shoes; polish; brushes; dusters.

Organisation: Whole group for introduction, small groups for washing activities.

Key vocabulary: Smell, clean, dirty, soap, bubbles, rub, polish, wring, wet, dry.

What to do: Explain that you are going to hold a 'Smelly socks day', and invite them to bring in a pair of socks to wash. Talk about the smells they are likely to experience – dirty feet, smelly socks, mud, soap, clean laundry.

Set up a laundry area in the role-play corner with warm soapy water in the water tray and washing boards so that the children can rub their socks clean. Provide rubber gloves for children with sensitive skin. Use a basin with clean water to rinse out the soap. Help children to wring their socks, put them through the mangle, and hang them up to dry. Talk about how, in the past, before washing machines, all clothes washing was done like this.

Open a shoe shine stall so that children can learn how to polish and enjoy the smell of clean shoes. Offer this as a service to parents when they come to fetch children at the end of the session and at the 'Senses factory' (see Theme 6).

Activity: Goodness gracious what a nose!

Learning opportunity: Moving around the room like elephants, balancing and responding to music.

Early Learning Goal: Physical Development. Moving and handling.

Resources: Large space; *This Little Puffin*; 'The Elephant' from *Carnival of the Animals* by Saint Saens; skipping ropes; playground chalk; balancing beams.

Organisation: Whole group.

Key vocabulary: Words of rhyme, big, slow, trunk, nose, balancing.

What to do: Ask children to find a space in the hall. Sing and act out the rhyme 'An elephant goes like this and that', from *This Little Puffin*. How big can they make their bodies? Can they make their arms into long trunks.

Listen to 'The Elephant'. Ask children to move around the room as they imagine an elephant would move. Collect words to describe the movement – slow, lumbering, swinging, careful, plodding and so on.

Teach children the song 'One grey elephant balancing', from *This Little Puffin*. Stretch out skipping ropes on the floor for children to balance on step by step as they sing. How many elephants can balance on each rope? Draw a spider's web shape on the floor using chalk and assemble all the elephants together to balance. What happens if the web breaks?

Display

Take photographs of children on 'Smelly socks day' doing all the different activities. Mount and display them for parents to see. Ask children to draw and write about the day on sock-shaped pieces of paper. Hang their work on a washing line with clothes pegs.

Theme 5: Tasting tongues

Teach children not to smell or taste strange things unless an adult has told them it is safe to do so.

Communication and Language

- Make a collection of words to describe tastes – hot, cold, sour, sweet, bitter, spicy, bland, tasty, nasty, sickly, scrumptious, delicious, tangy, smoky, salty, crispy, and so on. Encourage children to use these words at snack and meal times. (CL1, 3)
- Read or tell the traditional story of 'The gingerbread man' (see activity opposite). (CL1, 3)

Physical Development

- Use empty food packets, boxes and containers to build large-scale models such as walls, castles, machines and vehicles. (PD1)
- Choose four contrasting tastes, such as pizza, fish and chips, roast chicken, and soup and draw them on sets of cards. Chant the words on the cards and clap the word rhythms. Ask children to clap or chant their words as they move around the room. Can they find anyone else with the same taste in food? (PD1, 2)

Personal, Social and Emotional Development

- Read *Oliver's Fruit Salad* by Vivian French. Share a variety of fruit with children. Encourage them to try some more unusual tastes such as kiwi fruit and pomegranates. Let children talk about the tastes they like and don't like. Make a giant fruit salad to share together for snack. Which is the most popular fruit? (PSE1, 3)
- Grow cherry tomatoes, radishes, rocket or herbs in grow bags for children to try different tastes. Draw up a rota to help with watering the plants. (PSE3)

Literacy

- Make menus and posters for the Tasty Cafe (see Mathematics, below). Can the children choose their favourite meals and drinks for the menu. Help them to use phonic knowledge to write the words. (L2)
- Research, read and write recipes for favourite food to make at your setting. Let children choose favourite sandwich fillings and write simple instructions for how to make them. (L1, 2)

Mathematics

- Open a Tasty Cafe in the role-play area. Plan different menus, such as sweet, savoury, fruit, healthy, chocolate, and celebration. Make, buy and sell food in the cafe. Ask children to take on the roles of waiter, chef, customer, manager. (M1, 2)
- Play 'Eat the pie' (see activity opposite). (M1)
- Sing lots of number rhymes, such as 'Ten fat sausages', 'Five fat peas', 'Five currant buns', 'Five sticky toffee apples', etc. Can children make up new food rhymes? (M1)
- Sprinkle cress seeds onto paper towels in the shape of different numbers. How many numbers can they grow? Water regularly and then eat the cress in sandwiches or add to a salad for a snack. (M1)
- Make fruit kebabs using repeated patterns of different coloured fruit such as strawberries, grapes, bananas, orange, etc. (M2)

Understanding the World

- Put a small amount of flour, caster sugar, salt and icing sugar into four containers. Ask children to dip a finger into each powder, taste and describe the contents. Try matching pairs by having four pairs of powders for children to taste and match. (UW2)
- Make your own fizzy sherbet. Crush together 6tsp. of citric acid crystals (available from most chemists) with 3tsp of baking powder (soda) in a small bowl or pestle and mortar to make a fine powder. Mix in 4tsp of icing sugar and put in a jar. Ask children to dip a finger in the powder and put it on their tongue. What does it feel and taste like? (UW2)
- Make some tasty food for the cafe. Use strong flavours. Try peppermint creams or chocolate brownies, tomato soup or anchovy pizza. (UW2)
- Make a collection of tastes from around the world for children to try at snack time, such as French bread, Greek olives, Italian pizza, Indian pakora, Chinese noodles, American hotdogs and Spanish oranges. (UW1)

Expressive Arts and Design

- Give each child an A4 card sandwich box. Invite them to draw or stick on pictures of tasty and healthy food for their lunch. Sing 'What would you like in your lunch box?' to the tune of 'What shall we do with the drunken sailor?' (EAD1)
- Make favourite meals by gluing collage materials onto paper plates. Try sponge chips, brown corduroy sausages, tissue paper peas and so on. Use to decorate the walls of the cafe. (EAD1)

Activity: The gingerbread man

Learning opportunity: Retelling the story of 'The gingerbread man' to explore drama and cooking.

Early Learning Goal: Communication and Language. Listening and attention. Speaking.

Resources: Any version of the traditional story 'The gingerbread man'; gingerbread man cookie cutters; ingredients (250g plain flour, 125g butter or margarine, 125g dark brown sugar, 1 small egg, pinch of salt, 2tsp of either mixed spice, ground ginger or cinnamon, or a few drops of vanilla essence, peppermint oil or the juice and zest of half a lemon or orange or 50g of cocoa).

Organisation: Whole group to listen to story; small groups to act it out and cook.

Key vocabulary: Words used in 'The gingerbread man' story, biscuit, names of ingredients and different flavours.

What to do: Read or tell children the traditional story of 'The gingerbread man' who ran away to avoid being eaten! Help children choose different parts of the story to retell and act out. Everyone can join in the refrain 'Run, run, as fast as you can. You can't catch me, I'm the gingerbread man'.

Explain that you are going to make your own gingerbread men biscuits but there is a choice of flavours and tastes – spicy, cinnamon, ginger, lemon, orange, chocolate, vanilla or peppermint! Try to make some of each so children can compare tastes.

Beat the butter and sugar together until soft and add the beaten egg gradually. Add the sieved flour, salt and chosen flavouring. Mix into a firm dough and chill in the fridge for 30 minutes. Roll out on a floured surface until 0.5cm thick. Cut out shapes and cook on a greased baking tray for 12-15 minutes at gas mark 5, 190°C.

Activity: Eat the pie

Learning opportunity: Playing a cooperative game to develop recognition of colours and numbers.

Early Learning Goal: Mathematics. Numbers.

Resources: Paper plates; six coloured segments of card for each child; rulers; pencils; pens; dice.

Organisation: Small group.

Key vocabulary: Pie, circle, numbers one to six, colours, turn, slice, segment, piece.

What to do: Explain that you are going to play a game using colours and numbers called 'Eat the pie'. Give each child a circular paper plate and help them to divide it into six segments. Write the numbers one to six on the slices.

Ask children to choose six different coloured segments of card and number them one to six. Place them on top of the corresponding numbers on their plate. Take turns to throw the dice and remove or 'eat' that slice of pie. The winner is the first to eat their whole pie. Encourage children to identify shapes, numbers and colours and use mathematical language as they play the game.

Display

Set up an interactive display called 'Only the nose knows'. Invite people to distinguish between the taste of apples and pears while holding their nose. Can they taste the difference?

Paint a giant picture of 'The gingerbread man' and ask children to draw pictures and write about the biscuits they made. Use the cookie cutters to print shapes on thin strips of paper to make borders for the display.

Try printing with fruit and vegetables using bright paint on black sugar paper. Use potatoes, carrots, cauliflower, apples, pears, oranges and star fruit.

Theme 6: Working together

Communication and Language
- Read *The 5 Senses* by Nuria Roca. Talk about how the children use all five of their senses as they explore nature outside, listen to music and cook in the kitchen. (CL1, 2)
- Tell a story using all the senses or describe the senses walk. Give children picture cards for each sense. When children hear their sense ask them to hold up the correct. card. Invite children to make up their own stories about the senses. (CL1, 3)

Physical Development
- Draw large symbols for each sense on the ground using chalk – such as eye, nose, ear, hand, mouth. Ask children to run to the correct symbol in response to your questions. 'Which sense am I using when I... read a book/eat an apple/have a bath/listen to music? Some activities may use more than one sense. (PD1)
- Work with clay or wood (see activity opposite). (PD1)
- Talk about how using our senses keeps us healthy. What happens when one sense doesn't work properly? (PD2)

Personal, Social and Emotional Development
- Talk about how the senses work together to tell us about the world and keep us safe. Go on a senses walk around the local area. Point out how children are using different senses as they look at their environment, listen to sounds, smell traffic fumes and pick up leaves. (PSE1, 2)
- Introduce the idea of the 'Senses factory' that will take place at the end of the topic. What preparations do children need to make? Which of the activities would children like to share? (PSE1, 3)
- Play 'Which sense?' (see activity opposite). (PSE3)

Literacy
- Take a head and shoulders photograph of each child. Let the children label their sense organs. Ask each child to complete a caption for their photo 'My favourite sense is...'. (L1, 2)
- Write invitations to parents, carers, friends and local schools to visit the 'Senses factory'. Make posters to advertise the event. (L2)

Mathematics
- Give each child a simple outline of a figure. Ask them to draw in all the sense organs and count and label how many eyes, ears, noses, tongues and fingers they have drawn. (M1)
- Involve children in planning the games for the 'Senses Factory' such as 'Guess the number of sweets in a jar' or 'Guess the weight of a teddy bear'. (M1, 2)
- Make giant numerals using ribbon, rope, chains, construction toys, and so on. (M1)

Understanding the World
- Buy a whole fresh fish, such as mackerel or trout. Let children look at the scales through a magnifying glass, touch the fish and smell it. Cook the fish and see how the smell changes. Enjoy the taste of eating the fish. Which sense did they not use? Ask children to record what they thought on a simple writing frame (see below) (UW2)

	Before cooking	After cooking
Sight		
Hearing		
Touch		
Smell		
Taste		

- Make some bread. Weigh ingredients, mix materials, knead dough, smell baking bread, taste it fresh with butter and jam. Record thoughts on same writing frame. (UW2)
- Go on a bug hunt outside. Observe small creatures using magnifying glasses and bug boxes. Handle them carefully. Investigate how other creatures see, hear and feel. Draw around each child's hand and let them draw on a picture of their favourite minibeast. (UW2)

Expressive Arts and Design
- Paint self portraits. Let children look in small mirrors and paint their faces. Don't forget the ears! Frame or laminate some of the paintings. Provide laminated sets of labels for the eyes, ears, mouth, nose and hands using a computer and let children stick them onto their pictures. (EAD1)
- Act out the story of 'Little Red Riding Hood', when the crafty wolf uses all his senses to try and catch a tasty meal! (EAD2)
- Make musical instruments that are good to look at, make interesting sounds and have different textures to feel. Make shakers using clear, ridged plastic drink bottles filled with coloured beads, buttons, sequins, assorted pebbles, coloured dried seeds and beans, and feathers. Shake, rattle and scrape to make sounds. (EAD2)

Activity: Which sense?

Learning opportunity: Sharing a game cooperatively. Developing and assessing children's understanding of how different senses work.

Early Learning Goal: Personal, Social and Emotional Development. Making relationships.

Resources: Collection of items or pictures to represent each sense, such as light bulb, torch (sight); musical instrument, CD (hearing); socks, soap (smell); apple, ice-cream (taste); glove, feather (touch); five pieces of card; five plastic hoops.

Organisation: Whole group.

Key vocabulary: Names of items and senses, turn.

What to do: Collect together items and pictures of a variety of things related to each sense. Ask children to sit in a circle. Place the items in the centre of the circle with the five hoops around. Write the name of a different sense on each piece of card and place one in each hoop.

Ask children to work together to sort the items into the hoops. Check that children can say why they think that is the right sense to use. Choose some items that use more than one sense to challenge children's thinking such as food items, flowers, animals, and so on. Do some items fit in more than one hoop? Invite children to find other items or pictures to include in the game.

A version of this game could be transferred to a table top for an interactive display or game at the 'Senses factory'.

Activity: The clay factory

Learning opportunity: Using all the senses to handle and work with clay or wood.

Early Learning Goal: Physical Development. Moving and handling.

Resources: A handful of clay for each child; clay tools; clay tiles or boards; items to press into clay; existing clay models, sculptures or pictures; small pots of water.

Organisation: Small group.

Key vocabulary: Clay, work, squeeze, soften, roll, flatten, twist, press, pot.

What to do: Explain to children that in the clay factory they are encouraged to use their senses to enjoy working with

clay. Invite them to feel and describe the clay (cold, damp, hard) as they begin to work. Show how to soften the clay by dropping it onto a hard surface. They can squeeze it in their hands and flatten it by hitting the clay with the palm of the other hand; poke holes in it with fingers and draw lines with fingernails; roll into worm shapes and flatten with rolling pins; smooth the surface of the clay using small amounts of water.

Ask children to smell the clay on their hands. What does it smell like? Does the smell change when the clay is wet?

Ask children to listen, as they work with the clay, to the sounds it makes. Can they describe any of the sounds?

Encourage children to flatten the clay into tiles or leaf shapes using the palms of their hands and use tools to make patterns. They can scratch their names or initials into the clay.

Make pinch pots using a small ball of clay. Push the thumb into the ball to make a hole and pinch the clay all around the edges between the finger and thumb. Tap on the board to flatten the base. Rub with water to smooth the sides and insides.

Make simple model animal sculptures of hedgehogs or snails.

Any of these clay items can be glazed and fired in a kiln if available to make them last longer. Adapt the pinch pots to become candle or tea-light holders. Decorate with pasta, beads and pressed patterns and spray silver or gold.

Display

Mount and display the children's favourite sense photographs in a gallery for parents to see at the 'Senses factory'. Make a cardboard model of a child to stand and welcome visitors to the 'Senses factory'. On thick card draw round a child, with their hand extended, to point at the entrance, paint on clothes and cut out.

Bringing it all together

Explain to children that in a few days time you're going to be holding a special event. They can show their friends and families their work on the senses by opening a 'Senses factory'. Encourage children to think about some of the songs, activities, games and investigations they have enjoyed during the previous weeks. What would they like to show their visitors? How could they ask them to join in?

Preparation
Talk about making invitations and posters to advertise the 'Senses factory'. What information will people need to know? Who will they choose to invite? Don't forget to send invitations to other local schools and nursery groups. Adult help will be essential to the success of this event. Support will be needed in setting up activities, serving refreshments, manning stalls, taking photographs and helping children to enjoy the activities.

Rehearse the songs and drama that the children choose to show their visitors.

Refreshments
Ask children to think about which food would be suitable to serve at the 'Senses factory'. This could include:
- Homemade bread (see Theme 6)
- Different flavoured gingerbread men biscuits (see Theme 5)
- Tastes from around the world (see Theme 5)
- Noisy snacks: crisps, apples, raw carrots and celery, crackers and cheese, rice cakes
- Brightly coloured drinks: pink lemonade (add blackcurrant cordial to lemonade), blue apple juice (add a few drops of food colouring!).

Activities
- Set up five different sense stations around the room for children and their families to visit.
  Sight: microscope, kaleidoscope, magnifying glass, prism, mirror. Invite parents to touch Braille books and embossed letters and patterns children have created (see Theme 1).
  Hearing: bells, whistles, other musical instruments, spoons, CD player, iPod. Demonstrate the homemade telephone and listening tube. Play 'Musical moves' (see Theme 2).
  Touch: sandpaper, clay, dough, ice, finger paints, trays of sand or lentils. Display the children's feely boxes. Play 'Matching pairs' (see Theme 3).
  Smell: vanilla essence, perfume, flowers, chocolate, spices. Use smelly playdough and play 'Smelly matching pairs' (see Theme 4).
  Taste: jelly beans, fruit salad, salty crisps, pickles, tomatoes. Play 'Eat the pie' (see Theme 5).
- Play the 'Which sense?' game (see Theme 6) with children and visitors to see how well everyone knows their senses.

Games and stalls
Here are some more ideas for games and stalls that could be included in the 'Senses factory'. If a small entry charge is made, funds could be raised for your setting. Alternatively, you may decide to raise funds for a suitable charity.

- Guessing games: guess the number of jelly beans in a jar, the weight of a teddy bear, how many glass beads on a tray.
- Invite parents to buy framed self-portraits or photographs of their children (see Theme 6).
- Sell potpourri bags and scratch-and-sniff cards (see Theme 4).
- Display and sell clay models from the clay factory (see Theme 6).
- Set up a shoe shine stall so visitors can have their shoes cleaned (see Theme 4).

Follow-up activities
Ask visitors to fill in an evaluation sheet to show which was their favourite part of the 'Senses factory'. Children can look through these and find out which game or stall was the most popular. Put up on display enlarged photographs taken on the day of children involved in all the different activities. Ask children to compose suitable captions for them using a computer.

Resources

Resources to collect

- Large poster of child
- Glasses frames
- Senses books, puzzles, posters and games
- Braille books
- Magnifying glasses, microscope, binoculars, mirrors
- Shape sorters
- Large shell
- Story tapes
- Small jingle bells
- Different textured papers and materials
- Small cloth bags
- Small items for feely boxes
- Mangle, pegs and washing line
- Aromatherapy oils
- Spices – cinnamon, cumin, ginger, and so on
- Food magazines
- Grow bags and tomato seeds or plants
- Empty squash bottles.

Everyday resources

- Tissue boxes, cardboard tubes, plastic cups, film canisters, plastic bottles and containers, tins, art straws, paper plates, string, and glue for modelling
- Paper and card of different weights, colours and textures (such as sugar paper, corrugated card, sandpaper, silver and shiny paper)
- Dry powder paints for mixing and ready-mixed paint for covering large areas and printing
- Different-sized paintbrushes, from household brushes and rollers to thin brushes for intricate work, and a variety of paint-mixing containers
- Extra collage material such as lentils, beans, sequins, pasta, buttons, feathers, bubble wrap, cotton wool balls, different textured fabric (fun fur, velvet, towelling, blanket
- Softwood, hammers, nails, lolly sticks, bottle tops and paperclips for woodwork
- Salt and playdough ingredients and cutters.
- Glove and finger puppets
- CD player and musical instruments
- Role-play equipment for opticians and Tasty Café.

Stories

- *Lucy's Picture* by Nicola Moon
- *Duck's Key, Where can it be?* by Jez Alborough
- *Where's Spot?* by Eric Hill
- *That's not my Teddy* by Fiona Watt and Rachel Wells
- *The Three Little Wolves and the Big Bad Pig* by Eugene Trivizas

- *Whose Nose and Toes?* by John Butler
- *Oliver's Fruit Salad* by Vivian French
- *The Smelly Book* by Babette Cole
- *The Listening Walk* by Paul Showers
- *The Blindman and the Elephant* by Karen Backstein
- *Polar Bear, What do you hear?* by Eric Carle
- *Harold finds a voice* by Courtney Dicmas.

Non-fiction

- *The 5 Senses* by Nuria Roca
- *The Best Ears in the World* by Claire Llewellyn
- *Look, Listen, Taste, Touch and Smell* by Pamela Nettleton
- *Flip-Flap Body Book* by Alastair Smith
- *Senses* by Angela Royston
- *The Five Senses* by Herve Tullet
- *All About Me: My Senses* by Leon Read.

Songs and rhymes

- *Game Songs with Prof Dogg's Troupe* (Harriet Powell)
- *This Little Puffin* by Elizabeth Matterson
- *Bobby Shaftoe, Clap your Hands* by Sue Nicholls
- *Bingo Lingo* by Helen Macgregor
- *Me* compiled by Ana Sanderson
- *Noisy Poems* by Jill Bennett
- *Tasting Poems* by Jill Bennett.

Resources for planning

- **England:** Statutory framework for the Early Years Foundation Stage (2012) (www.foundationyears.org.uk/early-years-foundation-stage-2012)
- **Northern Ireland:** CCEA (2011) 'Curricular Guidance for Pre-school Education' (www.rewardinglearning.org.uk/curriculum/pre_school/index.asp) CCEA (2006) Understanding the Foundation Stage (www.nicurriculum.org.uk/docs/foundation_stage/UF_web.pdf)
- **Scotland:** Learning and Teaching Scotland (2010) 'Pre-birth to Three: Positive Outcomes for Scotland's Children and Families' (www.ltscotland.org.uk/earlyyears/). The Scottish Government (2008) 'Curriculum for Excellence: Building the Curriculum 3 – A Framework for Learning and Teaching' (www.ltscotland.org.uk/buildingyourcurriculum/policycontext/btc/btc3.asp)
- **Wales:** Welsh Assembly (2008) 'Framework for Children's Learning for 3 to 7-year-olds in Wales' (http://wales.gov.uk/topics/educationand skills/schoolshome/curriculuminwales/arevised curriculumforwales/foundationphase/?lang=en)

Collecting evidence of children's learning

Monitoring children's development is an important task. Making a profile of children's achievements, strengths, capabilities interests and learning will help you to see progress and will draw attention to those who are having difficulties for some reason. If a child needs additional professional help, such as speech therapy, these cumulative profiles will provide valuable evidence.

Profiles should cover all the Areas of Learning, as defined by the relevant UK framework, and be the result of collaboration between practitioners, parents and carers. Parents should be made aware of your record keeping policies when their child joins your group. Show parents the types of documentation that you are keeping and make sure they understand their purpose. As a general rule, documentation should be open. Families should have access to their child's documentation at any time and know they can contribute to it. Take regular opportunities to talk to parents about children's progress. If you have formal discussions regarding children about whom you have particular concerns, a dated record of the main points should be kept.

Keeping it manageable

Documentation should be helpful in informing practitioners, adult helpers and parents and always be for the benefit of the child. The golden rule is to keep it simple, manageable and useful. Do not try to make records following every activity!

Documentation will basically fall into two categories – observations and reflections:

Observations

- **Spontaneous observations:** Sometimes you will want to make a note of observations as they happen e.g. a child is heard counting cars accurately during a play activity, or is seen to play collaboratively for the first time.

- **Planned observations:** Sometimes you will plan to make observations of children's developing skills within a planned activity. Using the learning opportunity identified for an activity will help you to make appropriate judgments about children's capabilities, strengths and interests, and to record them systematically.

To collect information:

- Talk to children about their activities and listen to their responses.
- Listen to children talking to each other.
- Observe children's work such as early writing, drawings, paintings and models. (Keeping photocopies or photographs can be useful in tracking progress. Photographs are particularly useful to monitor children's development in the outdoor environment.)

Sometimes it may be appropriate to set up 'one off' activities for the purposes of monitoring development. Some groups at the beginning of each term, for example, ask children to write their name and to make a drawing of themselves to record their progressing skills in both co-ordination and observation.

Reflections

It is useful to spend regular time reflecting on the children's progress. Aim to make some comments about each child each week, and discuss these regularly with colleagues and families.

Informing your planning

Collecting evidence about children's progress is time consuming and it is important that it is useful. When planning, use the information collected to help you to decide what learning opportunities you need to provide next for each child. For example, a child who has poor pencil or brush control will benefit from more play with dough or construction toys to build strength of muscles in the hands and fingers.

Example observation sheet

Name: Lucy Field

Date: 17.1.13

Area of Learning: Mathematics. Count reliably with numbers from 1 to 20.

Context (Please tick):

Child-initiated: √   **Adult-led:**

Alone: **In a group:** √

Observation: Lucy is playing outside with two friends. She is trying to build the tallest tower and counting the bricks. "1, 2, 3, 4, 5, 7, 8. Mine's 8. Yours is only 7." She knocks the tower down, chuckles and starts to build again, counting as she places the bricks. "1, 2, 3, 4, 5, 7." The tower falls over. "Oh blow. I wanted to do 20."

What next: Check Lucy knows 6 follows 5. Encourage use of the outdoor counting grids, skittles and number rhyme CD.

Observer: E. M. Hogg

Overview of areas covered through 'The senses'

	Communication and Language	Physical Development	Personal, Social and Emotional Development	Literacy	Mathematics	Understanding the World	Expressive Arts and Design
Seeing eyes	Listening and attention Understanding Speaking	Moving and handling Health and self-care	Self-confidence and self-awareness Managing feelings and behaviour Making relationships	Reading Writing	Numbers Shape, space and measures	People and communities The world Technology	Exploring and using media and materials Being imaginative
Hearing ears	Listening and attention Understanding Speaking	Moving and handling Health and self-care	Self-confidence and self-awareness Managing feelings and behaviour Making relationships	Reading Writing	Numbers Shape, space and measures	People and communities The world Technology	Exploring and using media and materials Being imaginative
Touching hands	Listening and attention Understanding Speaking	Moving and handling Health and self-care	Self-confidence and self-awareness Managing feelings and behaviour Making relationships	Reading Writing	Numbers Shape, space and measures	People and communities The world Technology	Exploring and using media and materials Being imaginative
Smelling noses	Listening and attention Understanding Speaking	Moving and handling Health and self-care	Self-confidence and self-awareness Managing feelings and behaviour Making relationships	Reading Writing	Numbers Shape, space and measures	People and communities The world Technology	Exploring and using media and materials Being imaginative
Tasting tongues	Listening and attention Understanding Speaking	Moving and handling Health and self-care	Self-confidence and self-awareness Managing feelings and behaviour Making relationships	Reading Writing	Numbers Shape, space and measures	People and communities The world Technology	Exploring and using media and materials Being imaginative
Working together	Listening and attention Understanding Speaking	Moving and handling Health and self-care	Self-confidence and self-awareness Managing feelings and behaviour Making relationships	Reading Writing	Numbers Shape, space and measures	People and communities The world Technology	Exploring and using media and materials Being imaginative

Note: For each theme, highlight the Early Learning Goal areas covered through both adult focused and child-initiated activities relating to 'The senses'.

Home links

The theme of 'The senses' lends itself to useful links with children's homes and families. Through working together children and adults gain respect for each other and build comfortable and confident relationships.

Establishing partnerships

- Keep parents and carers informed about the topic of 'The senses' and the themes. By understanding the work of the group, parents will enjoy the involvement of contributing ideas, time and resources.
- Ask parents' permission before taking the children out on any of the walks. Describe the planned route and explain the purpose of the walk. Invite parents to accompany you.
- Photocopy the 'Family page' for each child to take home.
- Invite parents and friends to visit the 'Senses factory' at the end of the topic.

Visiting enthusiasts

- Invite adults who play musical instruments to visit the setting and play some live music for children to listen to.
- Contact your local branches of the Royal National Institute for the Blind and the Deaf and ask for representatives to visit and bring a working dog or show the children some sign language.

Resource requests

- Ask parents to lend or donate to you any old glasses frames (remove the lenses) or sunglasses, different textured materials and fabrics, an old-fashioned mangle and food magazines.
- Invite parents to contribute cushions and soft furnishings for the cosy listening area.
- Ask for volunteers to cook food from other cultures, favourite and national dishes, to bring in and share during Theme 4, 'Tasting tongues'.

Senses factory

- It is always useful to have extra adults at special events to help with stalls, games, activities and refreshments and to encourage and support children.